Printed in the United Kingdom

First Printing, March 2020

ISBN: 978-1-5272-6056-6

www.bank-of-me.com

Ordering Information:

Quantity sales - special discounts are available on quantity purchases by
corporations, associations and others. For details, contact:

info@theculturebuilders.com

This book is printed on FSC certified paper - we need
trees for more than just books.

FSC

-Thank you-

Here's to all the remote workers, all the people that juggle lives that are so much more complex than those most of us have. Here's to people who can keep their heads down and stay focused when all around them is chaos - noisy cafes, rowdy homes, cramped cars.

If you are already successfully remote working, this book is dedicted to you.

Like what you read? Sign up to our toolkit - regular doses of exciting content delivered to your inbox - www.bank-of-me.com

 united world schools

Ten percent of all profits from this book go to the charity United World Schools (UWS). UWS work in some of the world's poorest regions to give children access to free education by partnering with local communities and supporters around the world. UWS teach the unreached.

By purchasing this book, you are both investing in yourself and in the lives of many children.

www.unitedworldschools.org | Registered UK Charity 1129537

-Contents-

-Virtual Banking-

The first five chapters of this book are the main components of something we call Bank of Me™. It's a simple idea: thinking about our personal capacity - energy levels, drive, enthusiasm and emotional well-being - as a quantifiable resource that we effectively manage.

This 'human bank balance' is something that we all should work on maintaining at its highest level and, where we manage and lead others, support them to do the same.

It's particularly important to pay attention to it when working remotely: if we aren't intentional about how we live and work, we can become disconnected and distracted, ending up with a human bank account 'in the red'.

Our work with clients around the world involves shaping and guiding implementation of best practice to underpin high performance in these circumstances. The aim of this edition of the book is to give simple and straightforward inspiration to keep your personal and team bank balances high.

We hope that you can 'try a page' on a regular basis, and make some of these good ideas new habits that will boost performance in yourself and others in the remote working environment.

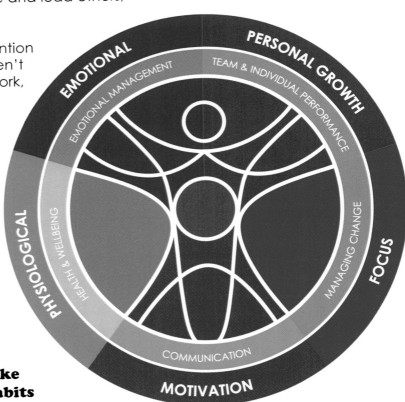

-Staying in the Black-

A key part of keeping a high human bank balance is to be aware of the things that send us into the 'red' with our levels of energy, emotions and enthusiasm, and those that keep us in the 'black' and feeling healthy, energised and positive.

Things that put us in the Red:

- Lack of purpose
- Sense that we are not valued
- Unhealthy diet
- No exercise
- Stress
- No ability to learn
- Unnecessary conflict
- Distractions
- Lack of sleep
- Worry
- Politics

Things that put us in the Black:

- Exciting work
- Great leadership
- Clear direction
- Down-time
- Eating well
- Achievable work
- Supportive teams
- Trust
- Knowing people care
- Learning
- Positive relationships

These lists are not exhaustive - there are plenty more things we can and do put into them to describe Red and Black situations. Feel free to add your own.

The trick is to recognise what puts you into these two states and, with some work, how you can avoid the negatives and build up the positives. When we are working remotely, we are far more 'at risk' of many of the factors that put us in the red - from raiding the biscuit cupboard to not taking enough breaks.

-So much to keep you busy-

As with the main Bank of Me book, we've stuffed this one full of resources and ideas that you can dip in and out of. Don't do them all at once, you won't manage it, and that's not the aim. We know remote working isn't always easy, and these are things to use when you need a boost or a way of focusing, remaining positive or pushing through a tough situation.

Growth for All

Finding Focus

Building Habits

You can also find more resources, tips and stories on our **Bank-of-Me.com** website.

Plus, we have plenty of remote working episodes on our **Bank of Me podcast channel** - available on iTunes, Podbean and Stitcher.

Got questions? Email us at **info@bank-of-me.com**

Bank of me

-Think about the 'third culture'-

'Your way' isn't always the right approach, neither is anyone else's. But there will be an approach that can work for everyone - what we term the 'third culture'. This is an intentional way of working together that you negotiate with your colleagues, attending to all aspects of your interactions. You'll need to agree areas such as how you communicate, collaborate, make decisions, feedback to each other, and manage yourselves: your energy, motivation and focus.

While we'd advocate agreeing a 'third culture' in any context (it applies for face-to-face working too), it's especially critical when remote working. So, think about which of the 'ingredients' of remote working you need to focus on for maximum impact.

And what are those ingredients? Some of them are the things in this book, but there are also lots of practical areas to focus on. Take a look at the wheel adjacent, it's a snapshot of the major areas of focus that are important for successful, sustainable remote working.

Some may be less relevant for you than others. You may be fully living some of them in everything you do. But, we'll bet, there are some that are under-acknowledged by your team and yourself, some that are maybe the grit in the cogs...

We suggest you use the wheel to plan your approach, make sure you think about all four areas, and choose the components in each that are most important to you now and in the near future. Then build your actions - work in the tips and tools throughout the book to ensure it's comprehensive and enjoyable.

As you read each idea in this book, you should bear this 'third culture' in mind. If there's an idea you like, discuss it, agree on how it'll work in practice, so everyone knows what to do and what to expect.

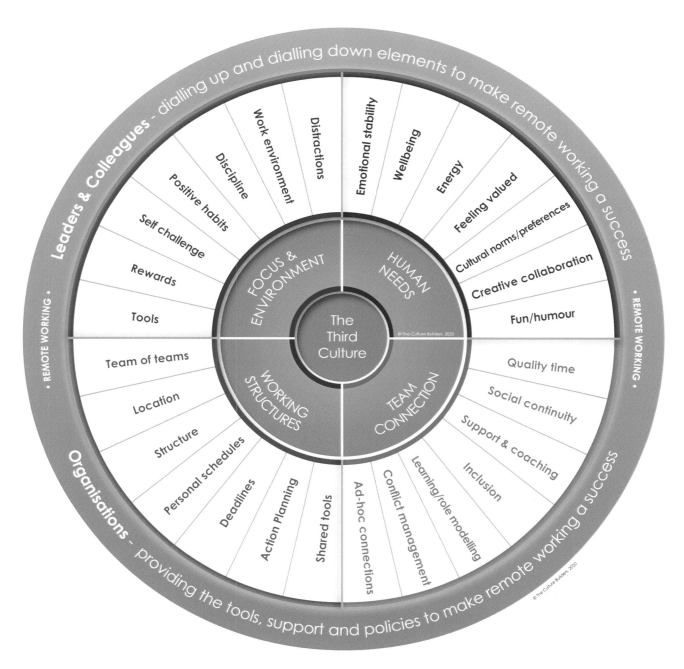

"Beware the barrenness of a busy life."

Socrates

Chapter One
-Getting Emotional-

Tackle the negatives, encourage the positives

-Getting Emotional-

"No man is an island" said John Donne. Indeed not - nor should we try to be, for that path only leads to greater problems (that second line is us, not John).

Remote working can be hugely isolating, and have a major negative impact on our emotions. Sometimes it's just a sense of isolation, as the situation disconnects us from people. At other times it's a real worry, anxiety and stress. Not a great mix, and one that needs proactive management to avoid.

Staying emotionally healthy is a life's work for everyone, and at 'peak' times we need to make sure that there's enough fuel in the tank to get us through and keep in the 'OK' space.

So let's not treat these too lightly, rather, let's recognise that we all have a responsibility to maintain ours, and others' emotions - for the good of us all. The tips that follow are even more important when we are (or working with) remote workers - showing value, appreciation and care is vital when people cannot see what is else is happening in our professional world.

Never be too busy to care about those around you... or yourself.

-Don't wait, call today-

Your social network closes down when you're working from home. You don't see all the usual people you would in the office. One simple little exercise is to close your eyes and think through how you enter and start the day at work.

You don't have that interaction now with all the people you would normally see. Rather than waiting for a time in the diary, just pick up the phone and give them a call. Well-being is that social sphere.

It's those little interactions that can put us in the Black or in the Red.

-'Fine' is what the weather is-

When you ask someone 'How are you?', very often the response you'll get is 'Fine'.

Someone once said to us, that 'fine' is what the weather is.

If we really did say how we were feeling, it would be very different, and could help us give and get the support that's needed.

On a good day we could say 'energised'. On a bad day we could say 'stressed'.

You are not the weather.

-Integration, not balance-

The phrase work/life balance drives us mad. The phrase tends to suggest that there is 'work' and there is 'life'... two separate entities, but they aren't.

You can't separate the two, work IS a part of life.

Think of your life as a pie chart and draw out the segments - labelling each one (mother, daughter, carer, community worker, best friend, colleague etc). What's the size of each one right now?

Is each segment the size you want it to be compared to others in your pie? Is the distribution giving you energy or is it depleting you? Is it withdrawing from your human bank account and putting you in the red?

What one action can you take today that will move you to the pie-distribution you want to see?

-Appreciation comes around-

Doug Conant, CEO of Campbell's soup, wrote 30,000 handwritten notes to his employees during his time as CEO - that equates to around 20 messages a day.

That was repaid to him during a time in hospital after a crash, where his wife read message after message from employees all around the world wishing him a speedy recovery.

Our three suggestions for making appreciation more meaningful:

1. Do it in a way that takes effort
2. Make it timely - don't wait to say it
3. Make it a habit

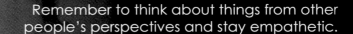

Remember to think about things from other people's perspectives and stay empathetic.

When things are difficult, great leaders make sure others feel heard and show that they understand how it feels.

"I've learned that people will forget what you said, people will forget what you did, but people will never forget how you made them feel"

Maya Angelou

-Valuing others-

How have you showed a colleague you valued them this week? Did you ask them for input or insight, or something else?

How can you ensure you show you value another colleague next week?

-Buck the trend-

We can never know what's going on for other people. We can never know what else they are carrying and how 'heavy' it is.

We've all been there, asking someone to do just one more small thing and getting a much more extreme reaction than we were expecting. Unless you ask, you can't know how somebody feels about what you're asking them to achieve, and that small, extra thing, might be one thing too many.

Why not do things a little differently? Ask an extra question or two about the capacity people feel they have before you load them up with more.

-Levels of social context-

Remember the standard amount of 'social context' expected in any communication differs from culture to culture. For some nations, things like challenge and speaking up are easy, but for others they are THE most painful things to do.

You might need to flex your style depending on who you're contacting, where they're based and what you're contacting them for - especially if you've not been in contact for a while.

-Shift the mood-

Be a postitive energiser, not a mood hoover

Instead of asking the same old questions when you talk to people this week - 'did you have a good weekend?', or 'how are you?' - or just saying 'good morning', try something new and see what happens...

'What are you looking forward to today?' or: 'What have you heard that is worth sharing today?'

Words Make Worlds.

How we choose to describe things creates an immediate and lasting impression on people - often it only takes one word to start a negative trend around something that was actually okay.

Canadian Airline WestJet has a saying: *"You don't get a job at Westjet, you become a Westjetter."* It creates a sense of membership and connection to something bigger than the individual. They also have 'guests', not 'passengers' - changing the way Westjetters treat people.

What worlds do you create with your words?

-The Twenty First Email-

When we work remotely, we use electronic communication even more that we otherwise would, so:

Look back at your last twenty emails in your 'sent' box.

What was the tone? What will the receiver have experienced? What course corrections will you make tomorrow to be even more positively impactful?

Now, having done this, turn to your keyboard and write the 21st one...

-Celebrate with stories-

'High performance doesn't happen by accident. You have to be intentional at recognising what goes well in order to repeat it in future'

You don't increase performance and spread best practice if you aren't talking about it. So get talking with your team and share what's going well. Celebrate each other's achievements and spread the learning that comes from great stories.

This probably sounds like common sense, but it's not common practice, likely because celebrating success with positive stories can feel a little uncomfortable at first, especially if they are about us and those immediately around us. Create a little space for your team to have a conversation at the start or end of your virtual meeting about what's going well, set the scene - it's all about making us better as a team - and kick off with a story.

I tried... the other day and it seemed to go well...
I saw you... and it had a great impact...
When we... we get great results...

-What would better look like?-

What is stopping you living a better life?

Wow – big question huh!

Maybe not enough time to reflect on that one right now, but ask yourself, what could I do today that would mean I live a better life than yesterday; that would put my human bank account more firmly in the black?

"He who has health has hope; and he who has hope has everything."

Arabian proverb

Chapter Two

-Culture Fit-

Nourish to flourish

-Culture Fit-

There's a remote working joke that says 'the biggest cost of remote working is the wear-line you make in the carpet when you go back and forward from your desk to the fridge'.

It's only partially true. Our health suffers when we work remotely and fail to take into account the impact on our bodies. A great deal is said about the conditions in the workplace, but little advice ever covers working from home or on the go. We are all guilty of it - too much screen time, poor seating arrangements, snacking on rubbish, not enough exercise.

A failure to take ownership of our physiological needs when remote working is a sure way to develop bad habits, with even fewer people around you to help keep you on track. This section gives some sound advice and ideas on better ways you can live your remote life.

Unless you are a magician, closing then opening the fridge won't make food suddenly appear. You are going to have to do better.

-Help yourself-

There's a lot you can do, physically, to help keep your positive energy levels up. Walk around - don't stay seated all day. Eat sensibly - not quick junk food. Stay hydrated - not just tea and coffee. But, we're not that great at doing the things we know help us.

A marketing exec we know sets alarms and diary reminders that say things like 'Get up and walk', 'Stretch', 'Drink water'.

You can do the same for anything that's healthy and that'll help you focus - remember that, without the visual stimulus or 'nudges' of seeing other people eat, drink, go for a walk, you're more likely to forget to look after 'you'.

-Like a breath of fresh air-

We need oxygen to survive, and while we're sure there's no shortage of that in your workspace, you still might find a breath of fresh air will wake you up, make you feel energised and help with concentration.

Open the window and get a breeze through. If it's cold, put on some thick socks/slippers and an extra jumper and do it for a little while anyway!

-System update ready-

What happens when your tech needs to update itself? It shuts down or restarts. Funnily enough, we need the same thing every day (and in smaller ways, more regularly than that).

Take regular breaks from technology throughout the day - it's just not healthy to spend eight to ten hours using a computer. And, at the end of the day, make sure you switch off any technology 60-90 minutes before you go to sleep because the light stimulates the brain and you'll find it harder to wind down/switch off.

Think about it like this...would you invite hundreds of people into your bedroom or living room in the hour before you go to bed? That's pretty much what you do by going on social media or news sites.

-Hit the reset button-

Without regular interruptions to break up the day (or a helpful co-worker reminding you to actually take a break), we're liable to keep working and wear ourselves thin.

Be intentional in taking some 'pause points' with little bits of meditation, relaxation or mindfulness. If you're not sure where to start, there are lots of apps that offer this.

Try to move every 90 minutes - and if you work remotely 'on the road', try to pull over every 120 minutes for air and movement.

-Grab an energy boost-

We all want to stay efficient and produce our best work all day, every day. However, we all have days when we feel productive and highly energetic and others when we feel slower and less inspired.

When you feel slower, distracted, or lacking in vitality today, try one of these five minute energy boosting activities.

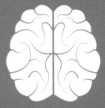

Jumping jacks or star jumps

A trip down memory lane

Watch a great music video

When you're sitting for large parts of the day, movement refreshes, motivates and resets. Get up and do a minute of star jumps or jumping jacks by your desk - it will get your brain back to firing on all cylinders in no time. Get your colleagues involved too for a team energy burst.

Research has shown that when we think about a time when we were really happy, we create positive emotions that boost our focus and productivity. Take two minutes out to remember the good times and the work you return to will definitely thank you for it.

Watching an inspirational, enjoyable, high energy music video is a great (and proven) way to give yourself an energy boost. Think about the music that inspires you and why. It'll largely depend on your preferences and interests. Link the team remotely and turn the volume up!

-It's not what it sounds like-

When you work remotely, you might not have access to a gym, or the hotel gym might not be somewhere you want to spend your time. A great excuse not to exercise, but come on, that's not you, you can do your own thing!

There's no excuse for not putting down a towel, pulling up YouTube and finding a home workout you can do in the privacy of your own room - let the neighbours talk about the puffing and panting sounds, you'll feel great!

-Breathe to micro-break-

The Samurai were taught how to breathe, first thing in the morning and right before battle and Olympians are taught to 'breathe like you are already the champion'.

Breathing 'properly' can have a huge impact on how we're feeling, especially when we are under pressure or about to take on something stressful.

Try this to reset in just one minute - it might leave you calmer, more focused and ready.

1. Find a quiet spot where you can sit or stand comfortably for one-minute without feeling too self conscious.

2. Close your eyes. Breathe in deeply through your nose for a count (in your head) of five seconds.

3. Gently hold the breath for one/two seconds.

4. Then breathe out through your mouth for another count of five seconds.

5. Repeat four more times.

6. That's it.

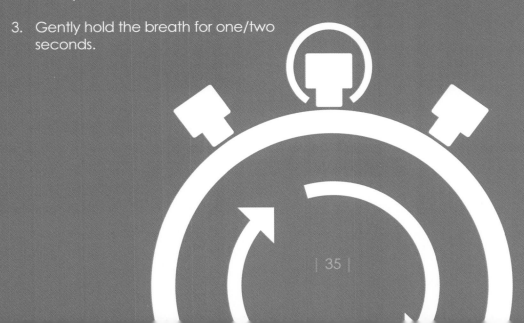

-Road snack-attack-

When you're on the road (or working from home) it's all too easy to eat and drink whatever you can get your hands on because it's convenient - unhealthy drinks, snacks and meals abound...unless you think ahead.

What trips and journeys have you got coming up that take you away from your usual workplace?

What food and drink could you order or buy today that would fuel you well? Think of things that are healthier options, but which you enjoy, to help you make good choices. Put some in the car/on your desk to combat snack-attacks when they hit.

-In it together-

It's a proven fact that having a workout buddy or team relying on you helps motivate people to exercise.

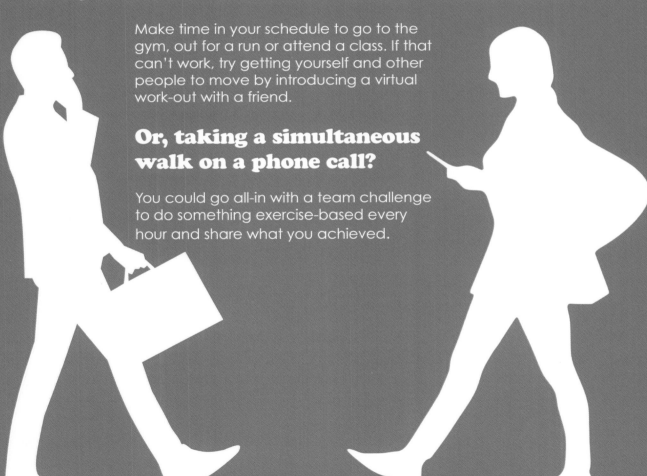

Make time in your schedule to go to the gym, out for a run or attend a class. If that can't work, try getting yourself and other people to move by introducing a virtual work-out with a friend.

Or, taking a simultaneous walk on a phone call?

You could go all-in with a team challenge to do something exercise-based every hour and share what you achieved.

-Use the 20:20:20 rule-

When we hear 20:20 we think of our eyes. We all know that staring at a screen all day is bad for our eyes.

Use the 20:20:20 rule (whether your vision is 20:20 or not) throughout the day:

Every 20 minutes, make sure you look at something 20 metres/yards away for at least 20 seconds...bonus points for relaxing your jaw and shoulders while you do it (we carry a lot of tension here).

-Sitting prettty-

Make your workspace as comfortable as possible - eight hours sitting in a bad chair isn't good for your body, attitude or productivity.

Also, don't sit in your bed working.

Keeping your sleep environment separate and distinct is more important than perhaps any other rule in terms of space usage and division. You do not want to associate your sleep space with work.

-Get the power-

If you're not getting the recommended seven to nine hours sleep a night then try to incorporate a power-nap or 'micro sleeps' into your day.

If you do take a power nap, set an alarm for 20-25 minutes. Anything longer might let you drift down into deeper sleep, which means you'll wake up feeling groggy.

Or, use Churchill's technique of sleeping sitting in a chair with your keys in your hand. When you start to fall into deeper sleep, you'll drop the keys and the noise will wake you up.

-Healthy separation-

Take the time to eat, away from your laptop or desk.

If the weather is good outside, try that, if not, try eating in front of the window and looking out on the world while you eat. To take it to the next level, try 'mindful eating' to slow you down and make you think about the food you're consuming.

"If you want to shine like a sun, first burn like a sun."

Abdul Kalam

Chapter Three

-Motivating Everyone-

Everyone on a mission

-Motivating Everyone-

Ah, the sweet cocoon of the duvet - it makes many of us question why bears get to hibernate for six months and we don't. That persuasive voice that suggests 'five more minutes' when we don't have to dash for a train or meeting can result in lost hours and an unproductive day.

'Lose the pattern, lose the pace' - remote working can be a slow slide into... well, not much really. There's a real danger that, when we remove ourselves from the hectic world of the office or workspace we also drop down a couple of gears in terms of motivation and drive.

As the old adage goes, if you want something done, give it to a busy person. And it's true. People who have a lot on their plate will deal with tasks efficiently, knowing as they do that more will come. Good practice is key here, with plenty of proactive approaches to structuring the day and keeping people involved and active.

The Devil doesn't make work for idle hands, he just gives them a smartphone.

-Watch the long-term-

"If you have a plan, you can hold it like a piece of acetate over the things people offer you, and you can assess the good, bad and indifferent of the fit and make conscious decisions rather than being swayed by others or a situation."

Steve Thorn, Executive Director at Civica

What's on your plan?

'There are hundreds of languages, but a smile speaks them all'

Smiling is proven to have psychological benefits for both you and those you smile at. It also helps people find you more approachable and relatable - even if it's on a webcam.

-A golden week-

"Was it a gold-medal day?" is a good reflection question.

But planning is just as important as reflection to motivate us into action. Knowing what you're aiming for, the biggest, most valuable goal you could achieve within the week.

So ask yourself, and your team, "What is this week's gold medal?"

-Being your best self-

We all know what it looks like when we're in our 'flow', delivering on-form, and being our best selves.

We also know what gets in the way of that.

Approach your manager today and create an opportunity to have a conversation with them before the month is out about how you want to 'show up' for the remainder of the year, **and** the areas that you want to focus on that often get in your way.

When that opportunity arises, share your thoughts with your manager. Ask what they notice in you when you're feeling and behaving at your best. Ask what they observe when you're maybe stressed, or in a difficult situation, and any negative behaviours start to come through. Identify three actions and how your manager can support you to implement them - and keep talking, don't let these conversations disappear because you are working virtually.

-Clear the work away-

When our work shares the same physical space as our home, the lines get blurred and we have to work hard to keep them clear.

Help yourself by tidying away your work properly at the end of the day - turn your living space back into just that, so it feels like a fresh, nice place to be.

Don't leave it and let it be a reminder of everything you've got to do tomorrow.

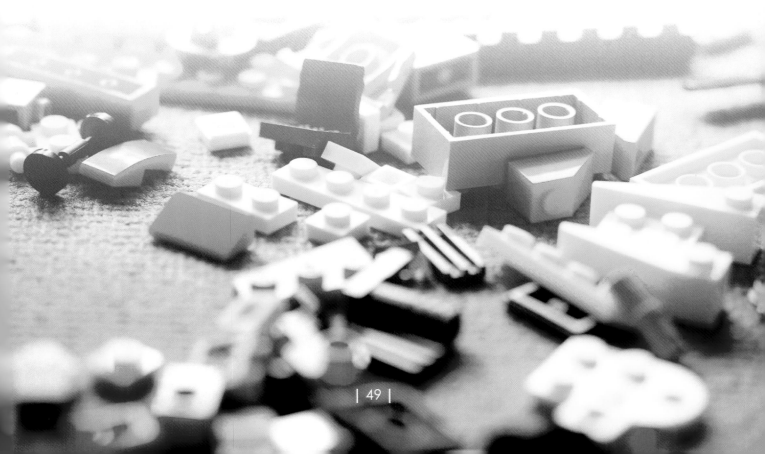

-Call in a sense check-

Perfection is the enemy of... Progress? Productivity? Good? Finishing things?

It hinders so many things and without a teammate next to you throwing a thought into the mix or saying "that's good enough", it's easy to keep refining things to the 'nth degree'.

Give tasks the time you think it should take to do them, then share them with someone for reflections and input - it'll stop you spinning your wheels and what you've done might well be 'good enough' already, meaning you've finished something else!

Rough edges on a first draft are OK.

-Lock(er) it away-

"Locker room" conversations are highly damaging to a team culture - both in what they contain and how they exclude people.

When people are not physically present, it's easy to drop them out of conversations and create 'in groups' of people who know and share more. Create space on the agenda to ask some critical questions; keeping the conversation in the group and in the open:

Has anyone got a better plan?

If there was one thing that could make this plan stronger, what would it be?

If one thing might derail us here, what would it be?

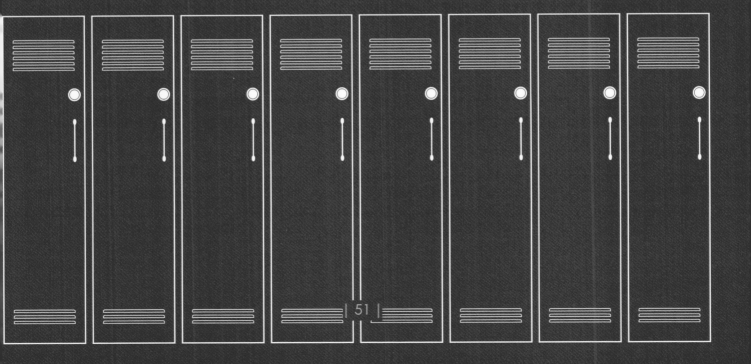

-Invest in creativity-

How can you encourage and enable people to be more creative for the next few weeks, rather than feeling like creative spirit is being dampened by a tough situation?

Take an action, give yourself, and anyone you manage, the challenge of reviving a creative talent that has lain dormant for some time?

(For one of our team it was rope weaving)

-Out of your hands-

If you know you struggle to get up and get started in the morning, don't leave it to chance. Arrange a call first thing (video or otherwise) with a colleague, direct report, your boss or just a friend, to get you up and running and off to a good start.

Starting the day early (or on time) gives you more flexibility and control over how and when you do what you need to accomplish before you stop.

-On the job!-

Not everything we do is enjoyable - far from it. Working remotely can often increase the feeling of a task being meaningless - no one there to give you encouragement or make the tedium go away. However hard it is, a great deal of development comes from utilising the opportunities a daily role presents - finding projects, stretch activity or developing new ways of delivering things - even when it's not as exciting as we'd like.

Try thinking about your role in three ways (and get your team members to do the same), it'll help show where opportunity sits:

Enduring
What isn't great, but you just have to do?

Challenge
what's really tough, but will ultimately benefit you?

Persistence
what's not great for you, but is absolutely vital?

Enabling
What is vital to both you and the wider company success?

Enriching
what do you do that adds huge value and depth to your role?

Fulfilling
What do you love, and delivers incredible value?

-Value other cultures-

Getting to know and respect wider elements of your team's local cultures around the world (and from a religious perspective) is essential. Simple things like observing each other's public holidays and local calendars are essential (knowing them is a good start so you don't arrange key meets on those dates). Also, take a look at the Levels of Social Context tip in the Emotional section for more on cultural factors.

Recognise important cultural celebrations too!

Inspired by 'Bank of me' by Jake Sparrow and Christopher Preston ©2018

-Action feeds motivation-

We often want motivation to strike before we take action, but the little acknowledged fact is that taking action breeds motivation too!

You probably have your version of a to-do list handy, but do you remove the things you've finished from the list once they're done?

You might want to think about also having a 'done' list for completed tasks... it's great for motivation to be able to see what you've achieved - and yes, we advocate making a note of the tasks that weren't on your to-do list but which forced their way into your day too!

-Shine a light-

What was great about this week?

What gave you inspiration?

Who were the positive energy givers?

Where do you feel you excelled in both what you delivered and the way you did it?

What does the plan look like for next week to be sure you are feeling good?

"A bit of fragrance clings to the hand that gives the flowers."

Chinese proverb

Chapter Four

-Growth for All-

Development people actually want

-Growth for All-

We learn the most from the tough situations and how we deal with them. Sometimes, it's a real challenge, and the last thing you actually want to do, but learning is there in every situation we make and encounter.

And it doesn't have to be hard-fought knowledge. We know that, when done effectively, remote working can free up time to try new things, to read and research more, to absorb information free from distraction and pressure. Using some of the other areas in this book - focus and motivation - there's a massive potential for you and your team to tap into - building new strength and capacity as individuals and a group.

For us, it's a double-edged spoon - on one end is the opportunity to learn and grow as you establish better ways of working remotely, and on the other end is the space and time to take on further learning (spoons are more positive than swords, BTW).

Any fool can waste time - heck, I've lost hours pondering this sentence. Learning, learning takes a brain.

-Love the 'tough love'-

When we hear tough feedback, the human response starts with 'ouch, that hurts', then we move to trying to 'blame' something or someone else, before finally hearing the message and stepping up. You can never get rid of 'ouch' and the desire to 'blame', but you can help people step up faster...

Remind people that you are on the same side and want to achieve the same thing before you put them on the spot and give them tough love.

-Curiosity vs interrogation-

When we're working remotely from others, it's easy for conflict to rear its head, and easier still for it to be left to fester.

Avoid conflict in the first place by making sure you're using the right tool for the task and are communicating well, but, if conflict does visit you and your team, stay in the moment and replace any potential accusations with questions to find out what's really going on.

-Impactful reflection-

We perform about 40-50% of our actions daily on autopilot, not through intentional choice. Bearing in mind the modern workplace, it's fair to assume a large part of what's left will be reacting to what's happening around us.

With all that going on, it's easy to forget the need to consciously reflect on the impact we can have, as colleagues and leaders, on those we interact with (even more so when they are not in the room with us).

Put a time in your diary at the end of the week to reflect on the impact you are having. Finish by thinking about the impact you want to have next week.

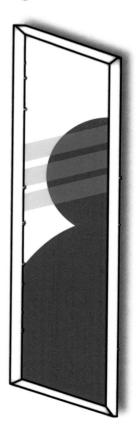

| 63 |

-Embrace the ridiculous!-

We've all been there (or at least heard the stories) when someone's child, dog, cat, or relative wanders into view on a video call.

Rather than let it be a source of embarrassment, embrace it.

Say hello, ask a question or two,
let yourself (and them)
be known!

It'll help grow your relationship too!

-Circle back on feedback-

Giving insight to a colleague (aka feedback) when you are remote, can be tougher. Follow these top tips:

Plan well - what words will you use, how will you be sure to land your point in a way that is helpful, when will you share the insight.

Remember - right intention, right place, right way.

Circle back - talk to your colleague again the next day to check their understanding of the insight and be sure it landed as you needed it to.

-Proxy connections-

When we share the same physical space, small, personable things happen that we don't even think about - like 'greetings' in the morning, and 'goodbyes' at the end of the day.

Try introducing **short** digital touch-points that replicate them.

A brief 'good morning' note telling your people how you are doing and what your main focus for the day is - and which asks them those questions...

A short 'end of the day' note, which tells people how your day went and that you'll soon be switching off for the night...

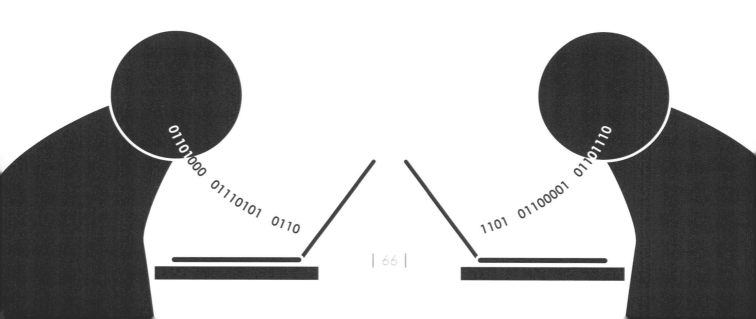

-The early (or late) bird-

Once you are getting settled into working remotely, start tracking your time. Figure out when you are most effective.

It might be in the mornings - in which case try to do all the heavy mental lifting in the mornings and leave the more "admin" type work to the afternoons, or use the afternoons to phone/video call people.

-It's not all about you-

If you're new to working from home, understand that it doesn't just mean change for you. It also means change for those you live with, your family, friends, or housemates.

Be upfront in talking about the new reality, how you want to approach it, what you - and they - might need. Revisit this stuff regularly to check on what's working and what's not.

-Knowing me, knowing you-

Convincing the people we work with that your point of view, argument, or idea is the best one is done differently in different cultures, and by different people.

Some like to know the background, reseach and journey to the recommendation, others want you to get to the point and tell them what action to take and how it'll benefit them if they do. Know the difference and you'll have a far greater impact - after all, it's one of the reasons our colleagues in America tell us to 'cut to the chase'!

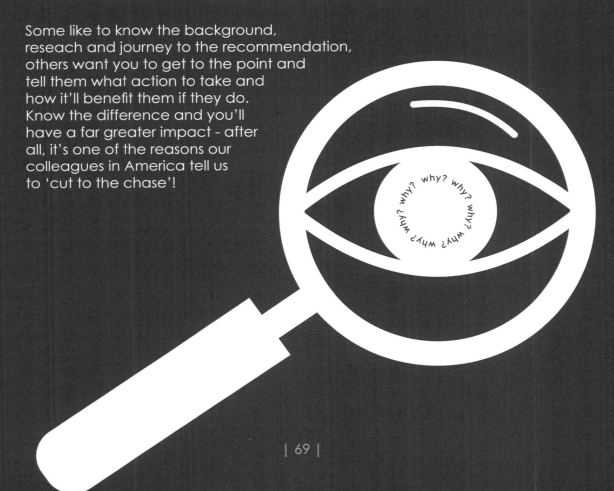

-Make the most of it-

Dealing with a new working pattern, and the whole host of emotions that comes with it, may be difficult - so ask yourself 'what can I control, how can I plan, learn and grow'?

If you're working at home, use the extra time you have from not having to commute to create a personal growth plan.

Get online and learn, chat to people you haven't had time for recently, tap into your wider network, read a book over breakfast, listen to a podcast during a walk.

-Time to upskill-

Every problem is not a nail!

Learn about the different tools available to you to connect with and collaborate with your people - know your tools and how to use them well.

Email is great...for some things...and when it's used well.

But there are lots of us that don't use it well, and lots of things it doesn't work well for...so try something new. Get to grips with collaborative, shared tools so you have the ability to collaborate, 'live', across distance and over time.

Find a learning 'buddy' and practice on video calls and shared tools - create your own sandbox.

-Keep talent close-

How are you connecting with talent - past, present and emerging?

Groundbreaking leaders make it their job to constantly connect with talent. They keep in touch with talent that have moved on from the business, nurture the talent within, and have a keen eye on who is moving and shaping the industry at all levels. Name the talent you've connected with this week ... how have you made them feel valued, shared a perspective with them or excited them about the future? Which talent will you ensure you connect with next week?

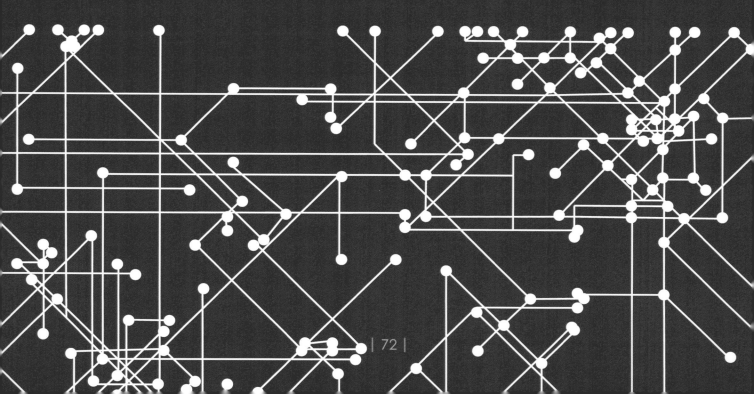

-Linking achievement-

"I can do things you cannot, you can do things I cannot; together we can do great things."

Mother Teresa

Who do you partner with to deliver your best results? How will you keep those partnerships thriving if you are working at a distance?

| 73 |

"Without great solitude, no serious work is possible."

Pablo Picasso

Chapter Five

-Finding Focus-

Do more... do less... do lots

-Finding Focus-

'Doing the right thing when no one is watching' is hard, but 'doing some work when no one is around' is even tougher. Finding focus isn't just a title that works as an alliteration - it also describes the practical act that many of us have to go through on a daily basis to be productive.

The challenge is, we live in a world that seems hard-wired to distract us, with everything attuned to trigger our five most critical senses. Conversations, good food, interesting content - it all puts a huge load on our ability to focus, which, sadly, we are not that good at.

Nature never really intended us to sit for hours doing one thing. We are not stealth or ambush hunters - we are hunter gatherers, and that actively encourages inquisitiveness, dispersed attention and rapid changes of focus. No caveman ever walked past a juicy fruit because 'slay mammoth' was his number one 'to do' item.

Focus is a social activity - we do it better when surrounded by people with the same aim. Sadly, at home, the dog or cat rarely has your level of interest in spreadsheets.

-Segmented hardware-

Research shows people have a desire to check social media once every thirty seconds, but that we are less likely to check social media if it takes more than 15 seconds to access it.

Help yourself to tune out from that desire by keeping your work computer for work and using it for work purposes only.

If you want to take it further, delete or logout from the social media apps on your phone so you have to put more effort into checking them.

-Café conversations-

Working when you're on the road means you end up with all kinds of strange and wonderful 'offices'.

It's quite common for people to find themselves in cafés, trying to do conference calls.

Remember that, while you might not mind the background noise of the coffee shop or your home - you likely won't be able to hear it through your headphones. But it can come down the line loud and clear, disrupting focus and distracting others - so use the 'mute' button appropriately.

-Swarm daily!-

Check in with your people first thing in the morning - try having a 15 minute virtual huddle to ensure everyone is ok, to check in on what they're doing and whether anyone has any issues or needs any help.

You could try swarming back at the end of the day to help close things down for everyone too.

-Be clear on boundaries-

Set up and maintain realistic boundaries.

At work when other people start going home it's a visual cue for us to prepare to leave as well. Working remotely means that there aren't those cues to tell us that 'work is done for the day'.

Identify the pattern that works for you and your life and don't apologise for maintaining it.

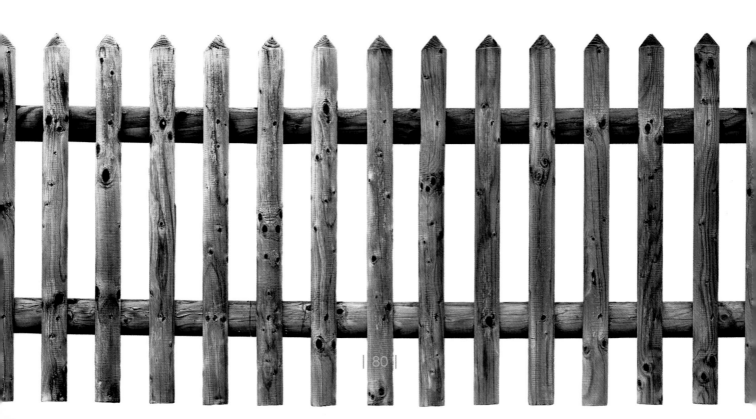

-The right tool-

What tools will we use to communicate and coordinate amongst ourselves and with the wider business?

Before each piece of communication, ask yourself if you are using the right method for your purpose.

-One thing at a time-

Don't do multitasking - it's often called 'multi-failing' for a reason.

So, avoid things like putting the washing machine on or starting on the ironing when you've got work to do, unless it's a reward after a 'focus sprint'!

Don't let chores distract you from being productive, after all, you wouldn't be doing them if you were working in a physical office!

(Also, don't answer the phone whilst ironing... old joke)

-Focus at every level-

Sometimes we need to help others focus on their own team, sometimes it's getting them to focus on being part of a team-of-teams.

How have you done both of these this week?

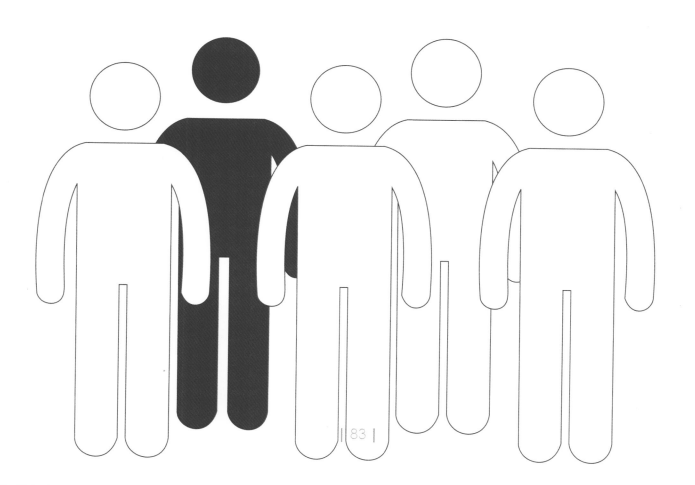

-Agree global ground rules-

Work together to agree 'ground rules' that work globally around communication (for meetings, emails and phone calls) then work together to implement them.

An example of this could be agreeing to rotate the timing of team conference calls so each territory takes their turn with the less sociable hours.

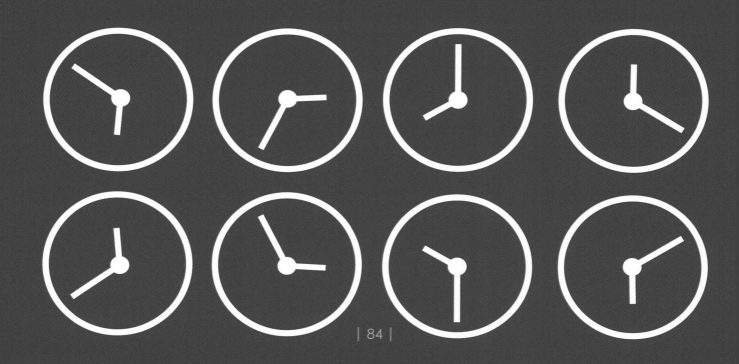

-Tell me something new-

When we learn new things about each other, it deepens the connections we have which has a great impact on how well we work together.

Make curiosity a part of your team conversation by asking different questions of each other in your next meeting - the more we know about someone, the more we can help them focus and achieve their outcomes.

Examples of questions you might ask include:

- What is your dream holiday?
- What is the most memorable activity you ever did with your family, or on your own, as a child?
- What is one characteristic you received from your family, or the people you grew up with, that you want to keep, and which one do you wish you could change?
- If you were stranded on a deserted island and could only bring three items, what would they be and why?
- If you could have any famous person over for dinner, who would it be and why?
- What quality do you appreciate most in a friend/boss/ co-worker?

Get the team to come up with their own too. Another idea is to have a 'virtual curiosity bag' where questions get picked out for each other at the end of each remote team catch up.

-Value your priorities-

What does the organisation or team need?

Is what you're doing today going to deliver against those two metrics?

If not, why not?

Be intentional with your time, energy and focus

-Decide how to decide-

The decision-making process can differ hugely from person to person, team to team and culture to culture, and is closely related to hierarchy.

Make sure everyone knows the who, how, when, and how much flexibility there will be on decision making, including whether decisions can or will be revisited.

This will iron out any cultural differences in expectations and processes.

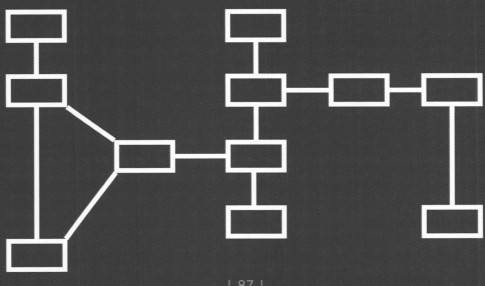

-Different timescales-

Some cultures (and people) treat plans and timings as no more than a 'guide' or 'advisory', while others stick to them like dogma.

Get clear on which elements you all agree are 'set in stone' and which need to be flexible to circumstances.

-Give the gift of time-

Focused time with another person is sadly becoming a rare commodity. Yet, when we stop and give somebody an hour, or a quarter of an hour... even just a couple of minutes, the impact is phenomenal.

Who would you give a gift of time to, and what would it look like?

A call, virtual lunch, or just face to camera time?

Make it something meaningful to both of you - a chance to connect at a different human level than perhaps happens day to day.

"Good habits are worth being fanatical about."

John Irving

Chapter Six
-Building Habits-

How to succeed at doing the same thing

-A good habit to develop-

Not everything in this book is designed to be a hard and fast habit - some things are ideas that you may try once or twice, when the need arises. Some, though, are actions that we would encourage you to build into part of your regular rituals.

Habits can also be the deciding factor for your virtual working being more than just 'OK'. They, when implemented successfully, can help you be a high-performance remote worker, one who is effective, in control and calm.

The crucial success factor will be the detail you put into your plan, and this is where the Little Thinking page that's coming up will really help. In our work, we see many people commit to a change or new habit creation, but then it quickly fall by the wayside. Their approach is too ambitious, vague or unstructured (often all three). Use the next few pages to make sure your habit is solid, practical and achievable - that you've got the support and the tools in place to make it happen.

Change fails because we love the idea of it, but not the hard work it takes.

-Hard habit to break-

What habits do I have that are getting in the way of me being at my best, everyday?

Take a moment to ask that question and reflect.

What can you do to create a new habit that would override the one that is less desirable?

-Caught by our emotions-

We can feel a little less 'in control' when we're in unfamiliar territory, whether that's driving somewhere new, in a new hotel for the night, or trying to work in a different venue.

'Nudge' theory says that visual cues are incredibly powerful at helping shape our behaviours. What small visual could you introduce that might help you stay empathetic and in control when things might otherwise hijack you?

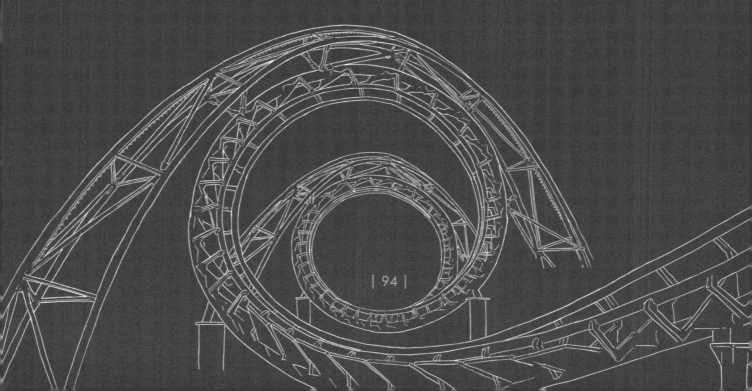

| 94 |

-Habits: Little Thinking-

We suggest that habits use the 'Six Honest' men that Rudyard Kipling made famous in his poem The Elephant's Child.

For each of these, you should have plenty of detail – they are all vital in ensuring you succeed.

What: What exactly is the habit you are trying to create – how would you describe it if someone suddenly you asked about it?

Why: You know what you want to do, but also ensure you are really clear on the why – why it's important to you and the team, and what the outcome of achieving it will be / what not doing it will cause.

How: What's your plan? What will you practically do, and when? What reminders will you use – diary, meetings, familiar objects in your life – this needs to be super-detailed.

When: Dates, times, time-spans, ensure you put in the detail to ensure you are clear what you are doing, and it fits within your life.

Where: Meetings, in your team sessions, at your home desk, travelling – be specific with yourself (think of a prompt or place that you could include in your habit to help you keep successful, for example, reflecting when you make a drink).

Who: Don't go it alone, get support by either involving the wider team, colleagues or asking others to be your buddy and keep you going on the journey.

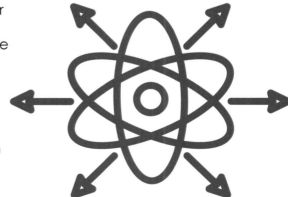

-Sources and inspiration-

Most images used in this book are reproduced under the Creative Commons licence (CC0). To the extent possible under law, uploaders of the images have waived their copyright and related or neighbouring rights to these Images. People are free to adapt and use them for commercial purposes without attributing the original author or source. Although not required, a link back to Pixabay is appreciated (www.pixabay.com). A small number of illustrations have been commercially purchased.

As ever, we need to thank our wider team members for their input, all of whom bring something to the mix and contribute their pieces of the book. We'd like to say a big thank you to them for sharing and helping build this resource - Steve Williams OBE, Jo Moore, Katie-Jo Stokes-Barnett, Beccy Matthews and Anna Jester.

Telling the stories of others always feels slightly cheeky, but we dutifully tell people we are going to 'borrow' them, and they never seem to mind. To anyone who recognises a story, thank you - sharing is caring.

We draw from our work with companies across the globe, some of which we have listed below. As with our first Bank of Me book, getting all the stories into one place was never going to work, so this volume adds new ones and fresh perspectives on what we hear, see and do.

Diageo	IBM	DAZN
Sony	BUPA	BBC
HSBC	Tesco	OVO
Pfizer	Just Eat	DAZN
Dyson	Clinisupplies	Salesforce
Asda	Starbucks	SSE Energy
NTT	UKTV	Lloyds Bank
Communicorp	Dyson	Edinburgh Napier University
Lane Crawford	Civica	Centrica
AOL	Perform Group	National Health Service

"Only Robinson Crusoe had everything done by Friday."

Anon.

-Author: Jane Sparrow-

Jane Sparrow has spent her career working with organisations across the globe to deliver transformational change and create high performance cultures. A published author, her leading book, The Culture Builders: Leadership Strategies for Employee Performance, has been acclaimed by business leaders, communication professionals and HR specialists, including endorsements from organisations including BUPA, Diageo and Starbucks. Her second book, Bank of Me; How to invest in yourself and others to build great cultures launched in October 2018.

Jane has worked as a special advisor to some of the world's largest and most respected brands, including HSBC, Glasgow University, BBC, Sony, Lane Crawford and NTT, to enable people to sustain high performance by nurturing culture and engaging people. Drawing from her experience working in senior leadership roles at Sony and IBM, she works with CEO's and local leadership teams to shape strategy, coach board members and run high-performance programmes. She is an expert facilitator, consultant, performance coach and impactful speaker that provides her opinions and insight to the global media.

Co-founder of the business consultancy The Culture Builders, specialising in transformational change, engagement and sustainable high performance cultures, Jane is passionate about enabling others to perform at their best to achieve organisational and personal goals. Her approach is grounded in the belief that by moving people beyond being simply 'savers' in an organisation and working with them to become 'investors' - people who will put far more in - organisations can unlock their performance potential.

Jane's work has also been incorporated into multiple university and business school curriculums, including MBA programmes and Henley Business School, where she was rated Henley's top speaker for 2016/7. She is one of a number of selected business and policy leaders, academics and influential thinkers contributing to the Prince of Wales's Business & Sustainability Programme at Cambridge University.

-Author - Chris Preston-

Chris Preston has been working in the fields of leadership, engagement and learning and development for more than 20 years, during which time he has delivered exciting, ground breaking work for global companies such as Transport for London, NHS, DAZN, Lane Crawford, Sony and Pfizer.

Co-founder of business consultancy The Culture Builders and co-author of the recently released and widely acclaimed Bank of Me; How to invest in yourself and others to build great cultures, Chris is a management and leadership team development specialist - both through multi-element programmes and more focused individual development interventions.

Chris is a psychology graduate, a member of the British Psychological Society, and a Level A&B trained assessor. This background came into good effect when he developed the company's core assessment approach – the Culture Builders Profiling Tool. With vast experience in psychometrics, including emotional intelligence profiling, Chris has worked globally with both public and private sector clients, building high performance teams to great effect.

Alongside this academic work, Chris is also well versed in setting up internal communications structures from scratch, and working on major, change projects – in terms of the communications element, the engagement with managers, and the practical approaches to embedding significant organisational change. Drawing from his experience working in senior leadership roles at Pfizer and global media company, Perform, Chris also works with teams spread across the world on effective, efficient and high performance global working.

Chris's experience and unique approach to designing and delivering leadership programmes and tailored content means he is regularly asked to run sessions around the globe where teams need positive challenge, new thinking and an inclusive style to bring out the best in them.

-Author: Owen Cook-

Owen Cook has been working in engagement & empowerment, personal development, innovation and change for nearly 15 years. He's worked with all sectors of the economy including local and national government, third sector services, and private sector businesses to help them collaborate with their users, customers and stakeholders. He's led programmes to drive innovation & positive change, to find and develop new and existing leaders through programmes, projects and coaching.

As Head of Programmes for The Culture Builders, Owen develops and delivers tailored approaches to tackle some of the biggest challenges in business, delivering them in interactive, enjoyable and practical ways. He's a guest speaker at Henley Business School on effective feedback and leads our programme development and delivery on effective management across cultures.

Owen spent eight years in the charitable sector - with four of those as managing partner of a Scottish charity and social enterprise - delivering programmes that had to jointly manage the goals of the charity with the aims and targets of clients, funders and government. Owen's extensive experience working with disadvantaged and disengaged people means he is practised in building helpful team behaviours, identifying and building motivation, and growing a sense of agency and empowerment through self-directed working.

In his work with The Culture Builders, he supports individuals, teams and organisations to live their values and perform to their potential. He draws in learning from high-performance business and sport, making it transferable to any context. He loves working with and helping people to grow.

As an expert in managing across international cultures, a strong extrovert, and the only member of our team based in Scotland, Owen is an expert in staying connected, healthy (physically and emotionally), focused and motivated whilst working remotely. Learning he brought to this new edition of Bank of Me.